IMAGES
of America

BROOKLINE

Character · Charm · Convenience

Brookline

This South Pittsburgh Development Corporation logo appropriately depicts in one place the essence of the community of Brookline. Visit the SPDC Web site at www.spdconline.org.

IMAGES
of America

BROOKLINE

South Pittsburgh
Development Corporation

ARCADIA
PUBLISHING

Published by Arcadia Publishing
Charleston, South Carolina

Library of Congress Catalog Card Number: 2004113373

For all general information contact Arcadia Publishing at:
Telephone 843-853-2070
Fax 843-853-0044
E-mail sales@arcadiapublishing.com
For customer service and orders:
Toll-Free 1-888-313-2665

Visit us on the Internet at www.arcadiapublishing.com

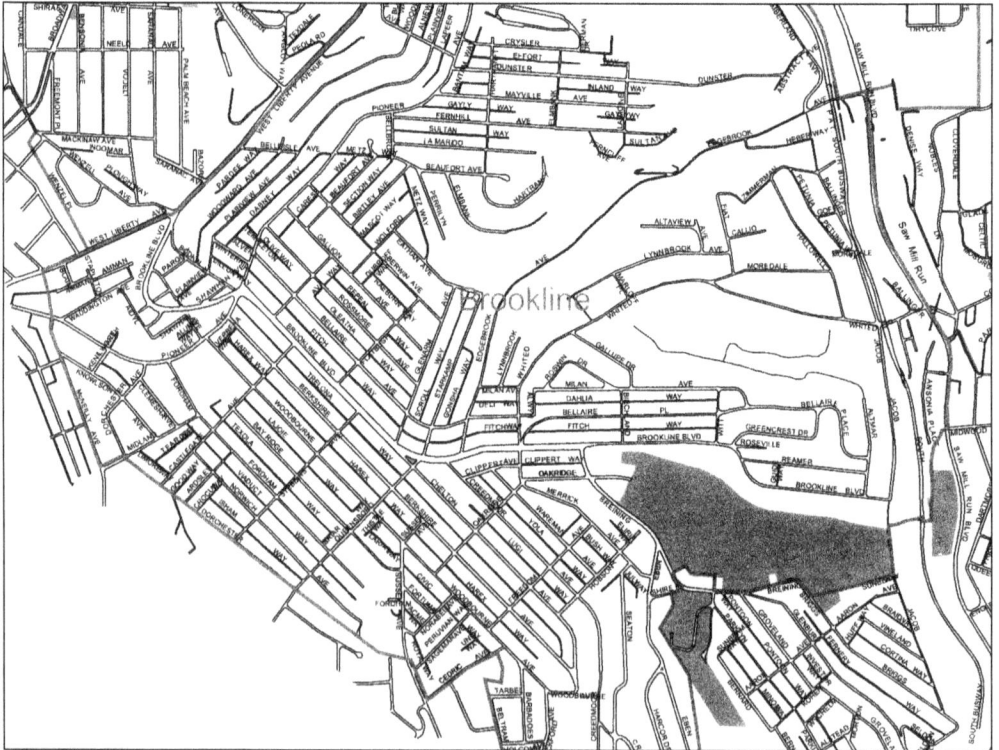

Above is a map of Brookline to help readers locate the streets and intersections mentioned throughout this book.

CONTENTS

ACKNOWLEDGMENTS

We would like to thank the following volunteers who contributed time and enormous effort to this project: Amy Fisher, book project manager and corresponding secretary for the South Pittsburgh Development Corporation; Clint Burton, who contributed most of the writing and research; Linda Dimitroff, president of the South Pittsburgh Development Corporation; Ginny Bell; Jan Beiler; Joanne Fantoni; Bill Feineigle; Annette Ferrieri; Harrison Flakker; Lois McCafferty; Dawn Miller; Mary Anne Miller; Ted Miller; Renie O'Leary; and Eileen Papale. Thanks also go to Pat Lorenzo, head librarian at the Carnegie Library, Brookline Branch, and her staff for their research assistance. A thank-you goes to the South Pittsburgh Development Corporation board of directors and advisory board, who generously supported and endorsed this project. This project would not be possible without the help of Pittsburgh city councilman Jim Motznik; Pennsylvania state representative Michael Diven; the Pennsylvania Department of Community and Economic Development (DCED); the Urban Redevelopment Authority (URA); the Mainstreets Pittsburgh Program; and the Community Technical Assistance Center (CTAC). Thanks go to Seton Center; the South Hills Alumni newspaper; Tom Mansmann; the Brookline 50s Picnic group; the Pittsburgh Post-Gazette and writer Bob Batz; and Brookline Boulevard merchants, businesses, churches, and civic groups for helping us spread the word regarding this project.

We extend our gratitude to our community contributors: Jim Addis, Bob and Jan Beiler, Clint Burton, Michele Capuano, Tom Castrodale, Bob Daley, Maureen Scanlon Block DeMase, Leo Demma, the Dimitroff family, Noreene Dooley, Mary Jane Doran, Edna Engel, Mercedes Faust and the City of Pittsburgh, Mr. and Mrs. Kenneth Fickley, Jack Flavin, Brian Fornear, the collection of George Gula from the Pennsylvania Trolley Museum, Shirley Johnson, Maxine Kaminski, Joseph and Theo Kirch, Bob Lewis, Mary McAbee, Elva McGibbeny, Doris Anderson Morrison, Ray Nagy, Kathleen Rebel, Will Saunders, Seton LaSalle High School, Ruth Smith, Helen Gallagher Southworth, Earl Sunder, Florence Bavilchak Tallert, Marian Tintelnot, and Ray Voith. Photographs were purchased from the Pittsburgh City Photographer Collection, Archives Service Center, University of Pittsburgh and also from the Library Archives Division, Historical Society of Western Pennsylvania, Pittsburgh. John Bromley and Michael Haritan are two professional photographers who allowed us to use portions of their collections in our publication. William Barrow, librarian for special collections at Cleveland State University, gave permission to use materials on behalf of the collection of the late Bruce Young.

Every effort has been made to obtain correct factual information and to acknowledge all contributors to this project.

INTRODUCTION

The community of Brookline is located in the South Hills section (4th City Council District, 19th Ward, and 32nd Ward) of Pittsburgh. Today, Brookline is Pittsburgh's second largest neighborhood. Throughout its long history, the community has retained a certain character and charm that has enriched its citizens. Along the way, it has built up a heritage that spans more than two centuries, back to the days when taxes were paid to the king of England.

The first settlers in the area were farmers and miners who served the needs of the Native Americans who lived on the land. The borough of Pittsburgh was chartered in 1759. Many of the earliest settlers were wiped out during Pontiac's Rebellion in 1763. After the American Revolution, the borough began to expand, and land grants were issued to veterans of the war. Those who settled here were mostly from the area near Brookline, Massachusetts. They named the region after their prior home for the abundance of small streams, which were common to the landscape they left behind.

The terrain south of Coal Hill (Mount Washington) was prime farmland, and for much of the 19th century, the area was dotted with small farms that helped feed the growing population of the city. Underneath the land, numerous mining enterprises and family-owned ventures tunneled into the hillsides, extracting the rich coal from the Pittsburgh coal seam to feed the city's burgeoning industrial growth.

The opening of the trolley tunnel in 1904 allowed fast, frequent streetcar service to spread throughout the South Hills. With the expansion of streetcar service by the Pittsburgh Railways Company to Brookline in 1905, residential development rapidly grew in the community, then officially a part of West Liberty Borough. Annexed by the city of Pittsburgh in 1908, Brookline continued to grow throughout the 1920s. This growth accelerated after the 1924 opening of the Liberty Tunnels and other transportation improvements allowed development to occur in areas beyond walking distance to the streetcar.

Brookline Boulevard, the community's main artery and home of the commercial district, was the central hub around which the neighborhood grew. It was similar to today's suburban malls, where most of the community's needs could be satisfied. There were food stores, hardware stores, doctor's offices, soda shops, shoe stores, dance halls, nightclubs, a bowling alley, and even movie theaters. For those who needed to travel, the public transportation network could get a person anywhere in the city.

The 1930s were a time of trial for all Americans, and Pittsburgh shouldered its share of the grief. Home sales and land development ceased as the country came to grips with the shattered economy. Pres. Franklin Roosevelt and his New Deal helped spur the nation to recovery. His Civilian Conservation Corps (CCC) program was responsible for the paving of many of Brookline's Belgium Block and brick streets.

The postwar years saw another spurt in the growth of Brookline. The country was developing rapidly, and Pittsburgh's steel fed that growth. New residential development in Brookline spurred another population surge. In the mid-1950s, displaced residents from Uptown and the

Hill District made up the last big wave of development as they migrated to the area around lower Pioneer Avenue.

The 1960s were a time of infrastructure improvements, expansion of the public and parochial school systems, and the development of community recreation facilities. Many roadways were rebuilt, and new lighting was installed. The streetcar tracks were gradually removed and replaced with bus service by the Port Authority of Allegheny County. Brookline Boulevard was paved all the way to Breining Street and expanded to four lanes. The population peaked at nearly 30,000 residents in the early 1970s.

The mid-1970s were a time of change for the city of Pittsburgh and the community of Brookline. The decline of the steel industry and the resulting loss in jobs caused the population to decrease for the first time since the Great Depression. In addition, the rise in popularity of the suburban mall brought many adjustments to the business community. Vacant homes and empty storefronts threatened to undermine the spirit of Pittsburgh's neighborhoods.

Through the efforts of many concerned Brookliners, and with the help of state and local authorities and local community action groups, Brookline survived the hard times and grew stronger as a result. Brookline Boulevard has come back to life, and the bonds that tie us together as neighbors have never been tighter.

Brookline in the 21st century is a vibrant community, with many activities and attractions for young and old alike. There are first-class recreation facilities such as the Seton Center and scenic Moore and Brookline Parks. The Boulevard is still a busy commercial hub, with many specialty stores and quality restaurants. Brookline's schools are among the leaders in the city, and the churches continue to inspire both their congregations and the citizenry at large with their focus on community enrichment and self awareness.

Brookline was, is, and always will be a special place for Brookliners everywhere. The community motto, "Character, Charm, Convenience," is the spirit that binds us as neighbors and friends.

The idea of publishing a book to capture the history of Brookline came about in the fall of 2003. There were many wonderful memories and much of the community's past to be found in files, folders, and storage chests. The South Pittsburgh Development Corporation (SPDC), led by president Linda Dimitroff and corresponding secretary Amy Fisher, sent out a call for citizens to contribute photographs, postcards, and stories of the past. The response was terrific, and the results are presented here for all to see.

One

THE EARLY YEARS

Brookline can trace its roots back to the Colonial days, when an old Native American trail known as the Chimney Town Road led to the McNeilly Farm, near present-day Castlegate Avenue. In 1788, when Allegheny County was formed, the region we know as Brookline was part of lower St. Clair Township. It was officially recognized as West Liberty Borough.

In the 1800s, the area was dotted with small farms that carried names such as Fleming, Knowlson, Paul, Hayes, Marloff, Sylvester, Fisher, Anderson, and McNeilly. Among the early commercial enterprises were Boggs Grist Mill, Marshall's Coal Mine, Kerr's Blacksmith and Horseshoe Forge, and Wilhelm's General Store. There was also Espy's Tanyards, where leather was supplied for boots, saddles, and harnesses, along with Beltzhoover's Tavern and the Bell House, where food, drink, and lodging could be had.

Pioneer Avenue was established in 1797 as a state road from Pittsburgh to Washington, Pennsylvania. It was later known as the upper road from Boggs Mill and also the Coal Hill and Upper St. Clair Turnpike. It was an artery of major importance, the only route from the south hills into the city. Wenzell Way, which led from Pioneer Avenue to Greentree Road, was laid out in 1832. West Liberty Avenue, along Plummer's Run, from the Bell House to Pioneer Avenue, near Potomac Avenue, was laid out in 1839.

The electric streetcar line to Mount Lebanon was laid on West Liberty Avenue in 1901. The road was unpaved until 1909 and was widened and improved in 1915. Whited Street is a former township road and, with the exception of a few streets, such as McNeilly Road, Brookline Boulevard, and the aforementioned streets, practically all other streets were created by virtue of lot plan developments, principally by the West Liberty Development Company between 1905 and 1908.

Early schoolhouses were located at West Liberty and Saw Mill Run, at Cape May and West Liberty, and on Edgebrook Avenue. The modern four-room West Liberty School was built in 1898, and Brookline School followed in 1909. Churches were equally as rare, with many citizens heading to a stump church on Pioneer Avenue and Brookline Boulevard to listen to a preacher tell gospel stories. The first organized church in Brookline was the Knowlson Methodist Church, built in 1868 at the Brookline Junction. By 1910, there were several denominations that had organized parishes in the neighborhood.

Trolley service in 1905 brought a wave of development to the area, and by 1907 West Liberty Borough was growing exponentially. Annexed into the city of Pittsburgh the following year and officially designated as Brookline, the area quickly transformed itself from a rural community into a modern city neighborhood.

The wedding of Barbara Hufnagel and Philip Fisher took place on June 30, 1889. The Fisher family owned a 17-acre farm on Edgebrook Avenue. Philip was the only son of Philip and Eva Fisher, who migrated from Germany in 1849. There were also seven daughters, including Mary Fisher (seated second from the right, holding her young child, William). Mary Fisher married James Anderson in 1874, and they started the Anderson Farm in East Brookline. This was a fine day in the life of two of Brookline's pioneer families.

Wallace Anderson is shown with the family horses in the fields of Anderson's acres. Wallace was the third youngest of the 11 Anderson children and the only to continue in the farming business after the sale of the family farm.

The Andersons pose for a photograph on the farm in 1904. Emma Anderson is seated on the horse to the left, with Phillip standing. Young Mabel is seated on the horse to the right, with Sadie and James standing.

Members of the Anderson family are shown in 1904. Sadie is standing to the left, and Emma is standing to the right. Phillip is sitting next to James, and Mabel is the young girl sitting between James and Mary. Young William is sitting in the front.

The Anderson family gathers in the mid-1930s. Matriarch Mary Fisher Anderson is seated at the head of the table, surrounded by her children, their spouses, and her many grandchildren.

12

This 1936 photograph of the Anderson Farm was taken from the fields nearest the top of Breining. The Andersons grew corn, tomatoes, beans, turnips, strawberries, and apples. The family subsisted on their own products and the abundant game in the nearby woods. Their produce and homemade products were sold at the farmers' market. Philip Anderson sold produce from his horse-drawn buggy on his daily rounds through the community. The surplus was taken to Pittsburgh for sale. In the distance are the 1400 block of Brookline Boulevard and the hillside homes that were built in the 1920s.

This photograph of William and Margaret Anderson was taken shortly after their marriage in 1926. William and his wife lived on the farm until its sale in 1945. They spent their retirement years living on Oakridge Street, on the doorstep of the new community center. In his later years, William would walk through the park with his great-grandchildren and marvel at the progress being made, and he delighted in the smiling faces of the community children as they played on the land he grew up on as a child.

Emma Anderson Schulze (left) and Margaret Anderson tend to the family cow. The kids always had fresh milk, and the rest was used to make products such as their delicious butter.

Making ketchup was another Anderson family tradition. The finished product was bottled and sold at the local markets.

Margaret (left), Emma (center), and William Anderson gather hay for the horses. Sadie, the family seamstress, made the hats that the women are wearing. They were made long in the back to keep the sun off their necks when they were out in the fields. The 20-acre farm was a rare piece of rural America in the middle of a modern residential community.

Pictured making apple butter are, from left to right, Sadie, Emma, Mayme, and Mabel Anderson. The girls would bottle the product and sell it to the local markets on Brookline Boulevard. It was a much prized treat and a big hit with the local population.

Adolf and Emma Anderson Schulze pose in 1947 outside their home, at 1331 Breining Street. Adolf was a Pittsburgh policeman who walked the beat in the Lawrenceville section. Emma worked on the Anderson Farm down the lane from their home.

This photograph, taken on March 18, 1912, shows the Estella M. Flanders property, on the west side of West Liberty Avenue.

The Central Meat Market stood on the corner of West Liberty Avenue and Stetson Street. The advertisement on the side of the building is for Ward's Tip-Top bread. This was also the location of the entrance to one of Brookline's coal mines, where local residents could get coal cheaply and reliably because of the Paul Coal Company's use of a revolutionary Fairbanks scale.

This view of Brookline Boulevard was taken near the intersection with Glenarm Avenue on January 17, 1933. The Kroger grocery store occupies the building that is now Chuong's Cleaners. At the time, Brookline Boulevard was the home to many grocery stores and small markets, such as Melman's Market and the A&P. The buildings to the far right were destroyed by fire in 1973 and have been replaced by the Mazza Pavilion, a low-cost senior housing facility.

Harry Grimm holds the reins in front of the firehouse in 1920. The engine house was motorized

in 1914, but they kept their horse-drawn steamer for several years as a backup to the fire truck.

Some of Brookline's earliest city firefighters pose in front of the firehouse in 1923. Harry Grimm is on the far left. The captain at that time was a Mr. Martin, and the hoseman was a Mr. Dalzell. These early firefighters were the first of several generations to be stationed at Brookline's Engine House 57. They risked their own safety to protect the lives and property of local citizens.

The firefighters of Engine House 57 pose on their motorized transport in 1929. Charles Smith (second from right) was the hoseman.

Two

BROOKLINE BOOMS

Brookline as we know it today came about largely through the efforts of the West Liberty Development Company, which transformed the rolling farmland into a bustling residential community. Prior to the addition of trolley service, Brookline was a farming community with only a few major township roads, mostly dirt trails.

The Pittsburgh Railways Company connected the South Hills to the city of Pittsburgh, providing reliable transportation and, as a result, increasing property values. Many of the local landholders divided their property into lots and sold them to the developers; the residential construction phase had begun.

Brookline was built in several phases. In the early 1900s, the original development (stimulated by the streetcar) was mainly from Pioneer to Queensboro. The building of the Liberty Tunnels in 1924 began a second major phase, as the convenience in driving into the city spurred an increase in property values. Again, the West Liberty Development Company went to work, this time in the East Brookline–Overbook area.

The Freehold Real Estate Company, which had a small office in Triangle Park on the small island that sits at the corner of Queensboro Avenue and Brookline Boulevard, handled most of the home sales. Construction was booming, and residents flocked to the suburban atmosphere in Brookline. Some of the best-selling home plans were, interestingly, from the Sears catalog. A home could be purchased through the big book and constructed by local builders.

While the residential development was in progress, the number of storefronts on Brookline Boulevard increased until the entire span was lined with multilevel shops and apartments. The many parochial institutions all had large churches built on or near Brookline Boulevard, and several schools were constructed, both public and parochial, to serve the growing population.

Brookline School was built in 1909 and expanded twice within a 20-year period. West Liberty School was expanded and served until it closed in 1939. A new West Liberty School was constructed in the 1950s. Resurrection opened its doors in 1912 and saw several additions built over the next 50 years. Carmalt opened in 1937; St. Pius, in 1955; Our Lady of Loreto, in 1961.

The two decades after World War II saw more change and improvement to the community. New residential development began, and infrastructure upgrades were performed. The community had completed its transformation into a modern city neighborhood.

The most notable change to occur over the last 50 years was the removal of the trolley tracks and paving of Brookline Boulevard in the late 1960s. With the exception of occasional additions, such as the Parkside Manor and Mazza Pavilion in the early 1980s and the construction of Brookline Memorial Park, the community has remained essentially the same.

An early-1900s topographical map of the South Hills area shows the lay of the land at the time. Where Brookline stands today is West Liberty Borough, and development is limited to the main roads: Pioneer Avenue, Edgebrook Avenue, Whited Street, and Brookline Boulevard. Things soon changed.

This is one of the hundreds of small coal mines that dotted the Pittsburgh region and the South Hills area. In the early 1800s, Pittsburgh coal entrepreneurs discovered the seemingly endless Pittsburgh coal seam. Mining enterprises sprung up everywhere to feed the voracious appetite of Pittsburgh's burgeoning residential and industrial base. Large companies and small family ventures all vied for the black fuel buried in Pittsburgh's hills. In the early 1900s, large mining ventures were in operation everywhere. In the South Hills, there were large mines in Castle Shannon, near the bottom of Edgebrook Avenue in Brookline, and on West Liberty Avenue. Many of these local mines fed the growing residential needs, while the major enterprises fed the industrial needs. By the mid-1900s, most mining ended in the South Hills area as the coal seam was pretty well tapped to capacity.

Pictured in 1909 is the Brookline Junction (the corner of Brookline Boulevard and West Liberty Avenue). Work has begun on construction of the double-track trolley line that will bring reliable public transportation to the community. The tracks traveled up the Pittsburgh Railways Company's right-of-way to Brookline Boulevard, which headed up what is today Bodkin Street. The right-of-way was widened in 1935, and Brookline Boulevard was diverted to its present route. The addition of reliable trolley service was a boon to the development of the community.

This photograph was taken at the Brookline Junction in 1910, when the single line service to Brookline was upgraded to a double track by the Pittsburgh Railways Company. The line was also extended all the way down Brookline Boulevard to the trolley loop near Witt Street. This was a major improvement for Brookline residents and led directly to the first real boom in residential development in the community. Beyond the intersection to the left is the old Knowlson Methodist Church, erected in 1868. To the right, at Wenzell Way, is a mining operation. An auto dealership now occupies the site of the church, and a McDonald's stands where the mine once operated.

This photograph of West Liberty Avenue was taken in 1915 from the intersection of Saw Mill Run Boulevard, where the Liberty Tunnels stand today. The railroad trestle, part of the West Side Belt Railroad, was soon upgraded as part of the new Wabash Railroad. Pioneer Avenue begins on the other side of the trestle to the left. The roadway was also widened during the abutment construction to accommodate the rise in vehicle traffic.

The Wabash Railroad abutment was reinforced in July 1915. A trestle was removed, and West Liberty Avenue was widened. This photograph was taken near the intersection of West Liberty and Pioneer Avenues. At that time, the Liberty Tunnels were still in the planning stage, so the trip to downtown Pittsburgh from this point took about another hour or two. People making the trip had to drive down Saw Mill Run, make a left, and go to the South Hills Junction, where the nearest incline hoisted their vehicles up to Mount Washington. They then had to take another incline down the other side. Today, the trip through the tunnels to Carson Street takes less than five minutes. Below, an October 1915 photograph shows the intersection with Pioneer Avenue after reconstruction.

The construction of the Liberty Tunnels began in 1919. The large steam shovels first stripped away the hillside, and then the tunneling began. The boring of the tubes was completed in 1922. By the beginning of 1924, work was nearly completed, and the new tunnels were opened to traffic. They were considered an engineering marvel; the nearly two-mile span was the longest tunnel in the country at that time. One unique problem was the issue of the ventilation of automobile exhaust. Motorists were passing out from the carbon monoxide that accumulated when traffic backed up. Vehicles were therefore counted, and tunnel use was restricted. Tunnel engineers worked with the U.S. Bureau of Mines to design a ventilation system, which consisted of two pairs of 200-foot vertical shafts that continuously pumped fresh air into the tunnels from a mechanical plant atop Mount Washington. The shafts were completed and operational in 1928, and traffic restrictions were eliminated. With only minor changes, the Liberty Tunnels have remained basically the same.

In these views, work proceeds on the Pittsburgh end of the Liberty Tunnels. At this time, further excavation of the hillside was being done on the Brookline end of the project. The tunnels had been in planning since the beginning of the century. One interesting proposal included a deep cut through the heart of Mount Washington.

Brookline Boulevard in Brookline at the Intersection of Chelton Avenue

East Brookline

*Many large homesites
on the carline,
80-foot Boulevard and
40-foot Streets running
back to 15-foot Alleys—with
protective building restrictions*

$30 *Per foot
front*   TERMS: Easy Payments
10% off for cash

No interest or taxes for one year

This real-estate advertisement from 1927 markets the new developments in East Brookline. The photograph shows the Freehold Real Estate office in Triangle Park, where the Cannon rests today. There is also a striking lack of trees along the sidewalk.

This marketing brochure for the Freehold Real Estate Company advertises the new car line, which opened development in East Brookline.

The Freehold Real Estate Company advertised lots for sale in Brookline with these descriptive and intriguing flyers. Apparently their tactics worked. Thousands of lots were purchased, and many homes were built.

Brookline Boulevard Showing a Part of the Business Section and Engine House

East Brookline

Paved · Sewered
Gas · Water
Every City Improvement
in the midst of suburban
beauty that is ideal
and conducive to
health and happiness

A Real Boon to Child Life

Another real-estate advertisement describes life in Brookline in 1927 as well as today.

This photograph shows the construction of the home of newlyweds Jim Daugherty and Marie Fisher, at 2037 Edgebrook Avenue. The Fisher family once owned 17 acres of farmland at this location. The Daughertys lived in the house until the late 1950s. The canine foreman in the foreground is Marie's dog, Sport.

The home at 1042 Bellaire Avenue was built in 1927 by James N. Addis and his brother Samuel. James and his wife, Julia, are standing on the front porch.

THE FULLERTON

This style of home has become very popular in the past few years. It adapts itself equally well to city lots or country estates, and in few other styles can you get so much space for such a small outlay of money.

Details and features: Six rooms and one bath. Full-width front porch with hipped roof supported by brick and wood piers; hipped-gable dormer; glazed front door. Fireplace in living room; open stairs.

Years and catalog numbers: 1925 (3205X), 1926 (3205X), 1928 (P3205), 1929 (P3205), 1931 (3205)

Price: $1,635 to $2,234

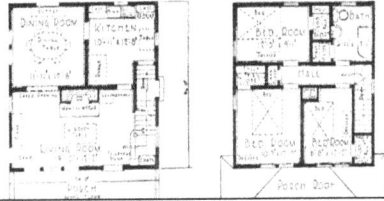

In the 1920s, a homebuyer could pick and choose from a variety of home styles offered in the Sears catalog. The materials were shipped to the location, and the home was built by local builders. The Fullerton was one of those designs. It was used to build this home at 1327 Oakridge Street and many other residences throughout Brookline.

The houses at 901 and 903 Norwich Avenue were built in 1920 and 1927, respectively. The Tintelnots resided at No. 903 when it was built.

Brookline Boulevard is shown as it appeared in 1928. Many people were purchasing automobiles in the 1920s, but there is something particularly interesting about seeing those cars on the street in front of buildings that are still familiar today.

This postcard from 1929 shows an artist's conception of how the Liberty Tunnels and the intersection of West Liberty Avenue and Saw Mill Run Boulevard could have looked.

Sussex Avenue is pictured from McNeilly Road during excavation in 1933. It was just a dirt path through the woods.

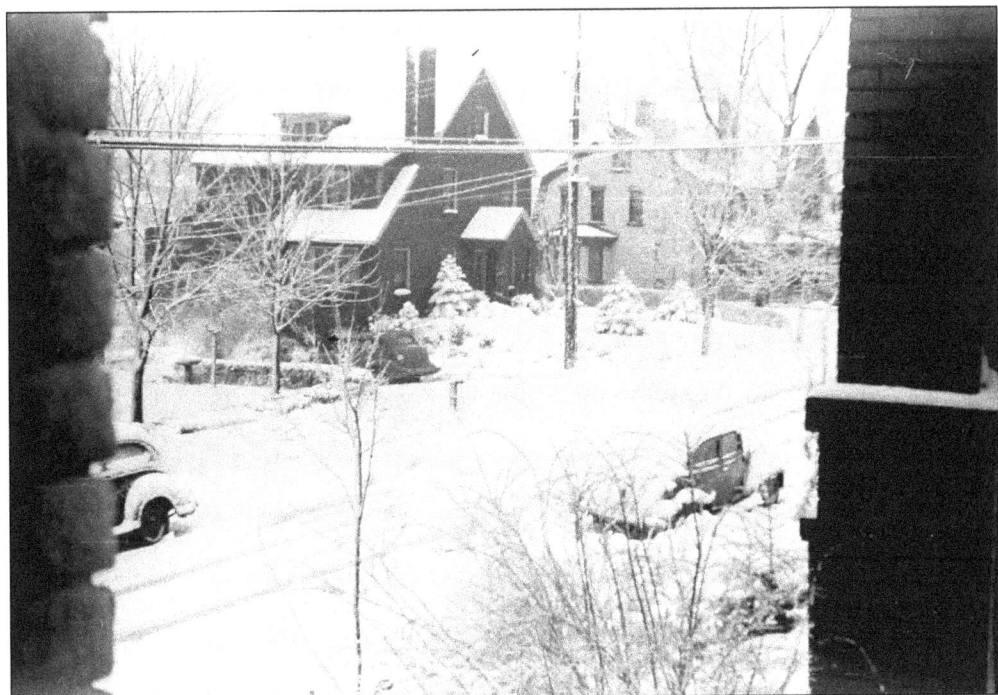

The 700 and 800 blocks of Bellaire Avenue, near the intersection with Flatbush, are shown after a snowfall in 1938.

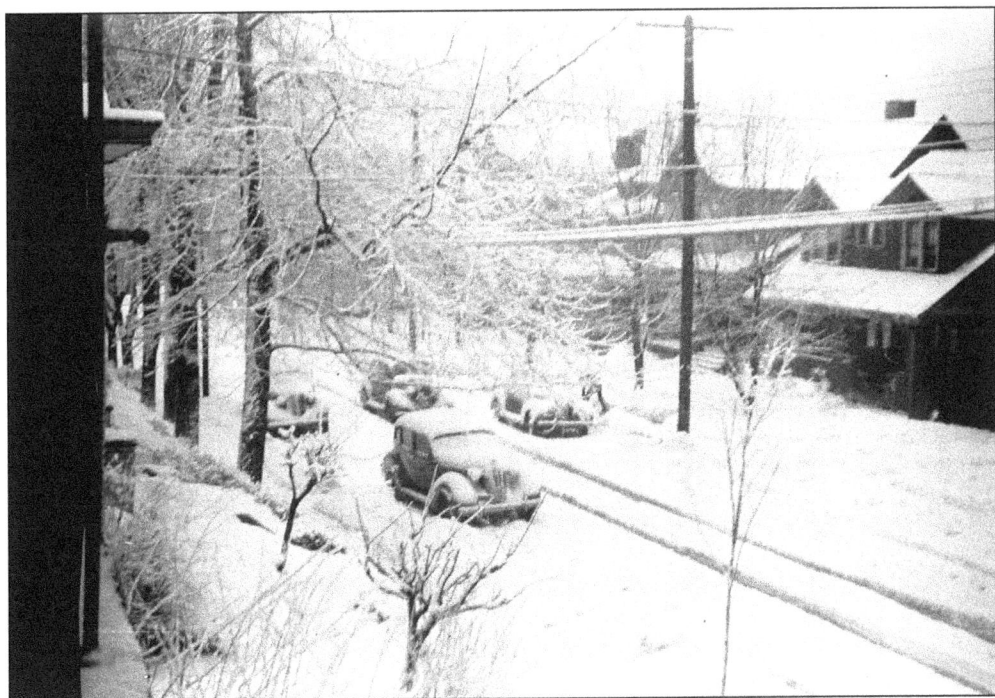

This photograph was taken from the porch of 809 Bellaire Avenue (the Voith family's home) after the big snowstorm of 1938.

Flooding has been an ongoing problem along Saw Mill Run Boulevard, as the creek often overflows in heavy rain. Attempts at flood control have been unsuccessful. These photographs were taken in 1938.

The house at 2306 Whited Street, built in 1939, still stands today. When this 1941 photograph was taken, it was the only home in the area, except for the Marloff Farm house (far right), which is also still standing. The same family still owns the house, now with a large addition. Lynnbrook Avenue was not developed until the 1950s. Other homes were built along Whited Street as the Marloff Farm land was sold off into plots.

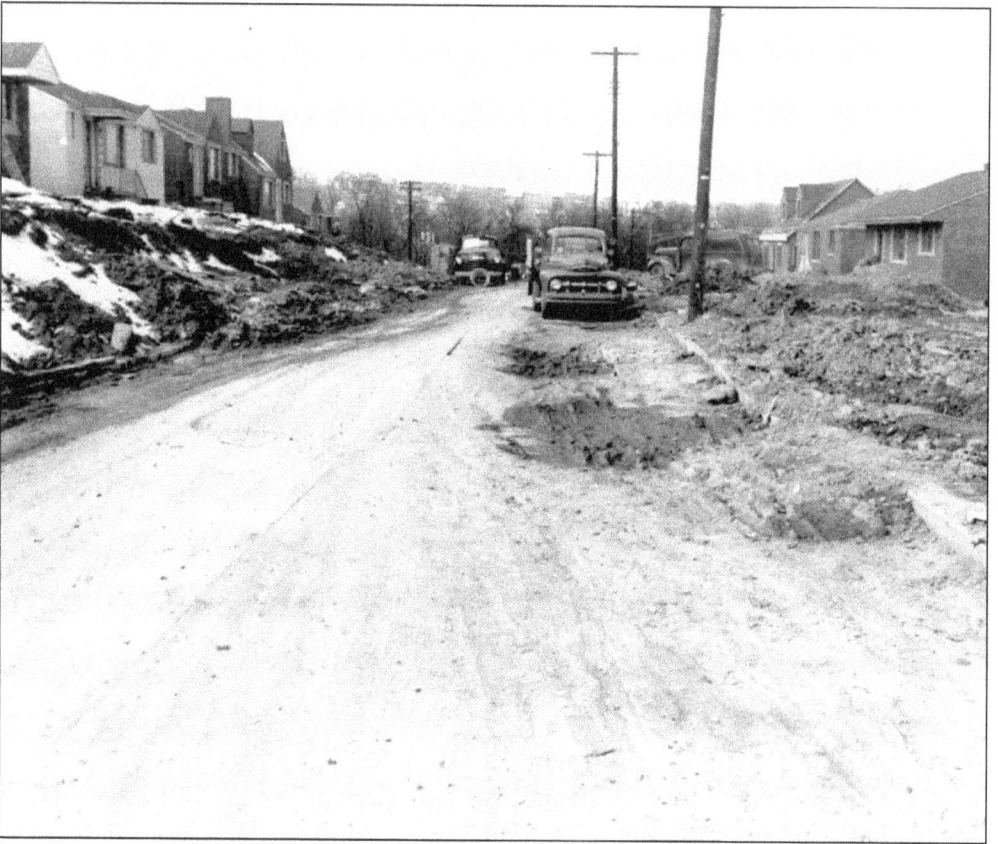

Northcrest Drive is shown under construction on March 8, 1954.

The intersection of Northcrest Drive and Pioneer Avenue is seen on October 7, 1955.

These photographs show the reconstruction of the 1500 block of Berkshire Avenue on March 11, 1958. Notice the lack of trees along the landscape, compared to today's view.

The upper entrance to the Brookline Memorial Community Center is pictured in 1963. It was formerly the entrance to the Anderson Farm. By this time, the community center was a beehive of activity. The home on the left, at 1331 Breining Street, belonged to Adolf and Emma Anderson Schulze. Emma was one of the Andersons who grew up on the farm. The house sits at the entrance to what was once her family property. She was delighted as her family home was converted into a park for the children of Brookline.

Seen on May 24, 1963, is the intersection of Ballinger and Whited Streets. Larry's Roadhouse Restaurant now occupies the old railroad boarding home (on the hillside to the left). The car on the left belongs to Pittsburgh's public works department. The sign on the right advertises S&H green stamps.

Breining Street at Shire Place is seen on October 16, 1963.

Breining Street is shown in a view looking toward Oakridge Street and Merrick Avenue on October 8, 1963. Formerly known as Ormond Street, the road was originally opened to two-way traffic. Today it has a one-way restriction.

Michael Haritan captured the essence of Brookline when he took this photograph of our typical

neighborhood hillside.

Richard Dunn (left) and Donald Fornear shovel coal on Woodbourne Avenue, near Freedom, c. 1943. The coal company would dump a load onto the street, and the young workers would move it into the coal cellar through the coal chute. Around the late 1940s, coal furnaces were converted to gas, but the coal dust embedded in the walls and rafters took years of cleaning to remove.

50

Three

TROLLEYS AND
TRANSPORTATION

Transportation from the South Hills to Pittsburgh in the early days was slow and difficult. Travelers got to the city by wagon or rode the narrow-gauge Pittsburgh and Castle Shannon Railroad, which followed the general course of the present Overbrook trolley line. Passenger cars were pulled up an incline from Beltzhoover and Haberman to Bailey Avenue on Mount Washington, and then passengers walked across Bailey to board the Castle Shannon incline to Carson Street and Arlington Avenue. From there they traveled by horsecar or by foot to downtown. In 1901, the streetcar line ran the length of West Liberty Avenue and extended to many South Hills communities. One single-track line was built to Brookline Boulevard in 1905.

At the dawn of the 20th century, almost all roads were dirt with few sidewalks. The heavy traffic (mostly horses and wagons) cut deep ruts into the roads, so the mud in wet weather was often axle deep. Pedestrians fared no better. Finally, Reverend Jones of the Knowlson Methodist Church (at the Brookline Junction) secured funds, with the help of a friend, to purchase boards for a boardwalk. With the help of the community, the boards were laid from the city line to the Old Bell House at Saw Mill Run and West Liberty. This was the first public improvement in the area.

Within a few short years, huge strides in transportation were made. By 1903, the Wright brothers' historic flight and Henry Ford's first automobile were actualities. The streetcar tunnel under Mount Washington was opened in 1904. This was a phenomenal breakthrough to the South Hills. It shortened the trip to town by miles and hours. It gave impetus to the West Liberty Development Company and other real-estate firms (between 1905 and 1908) to lay out streets and lots in the portion of West Liberty Borough that was to become Brookline.

The Liberty Tunnels were built in 1924. As with the trolley tunnel 20 years prior, they led to a dramatic decrease in the travel time to the city. With the population booming and residential development on the rise again, many improvements were made to the road network in the community. Most roads were paved, and modern sewers were installed. The tracks were paved with brick in 1936 from Pioneer to Creedmore Avenues.

In the 1960s, the trolley network was dismantled in favor of bus service. This led to the paving and widening of Brookline Boulevard, a major improvement over the previously congested two-lane artery of the past. Sometime in the near future, Brookline Boulevard is scheduled for a major facelift, one that will transform the highly traveled artery into a beautiful tree-lined boulevard with many improvements for vehicle and pedestrian traffic flow.

The South Hills Junction was new in 1906. This photograph was taken from a spot above the portal. The billboard to the left advertises lots in Brookline and 15-minute streetcar service. The steam trains were operated by the Pittsburgh Railways Company from 1905 until 1912, although the Pittsburgh & Castle Shannon Railroad had been in existence since 1871.

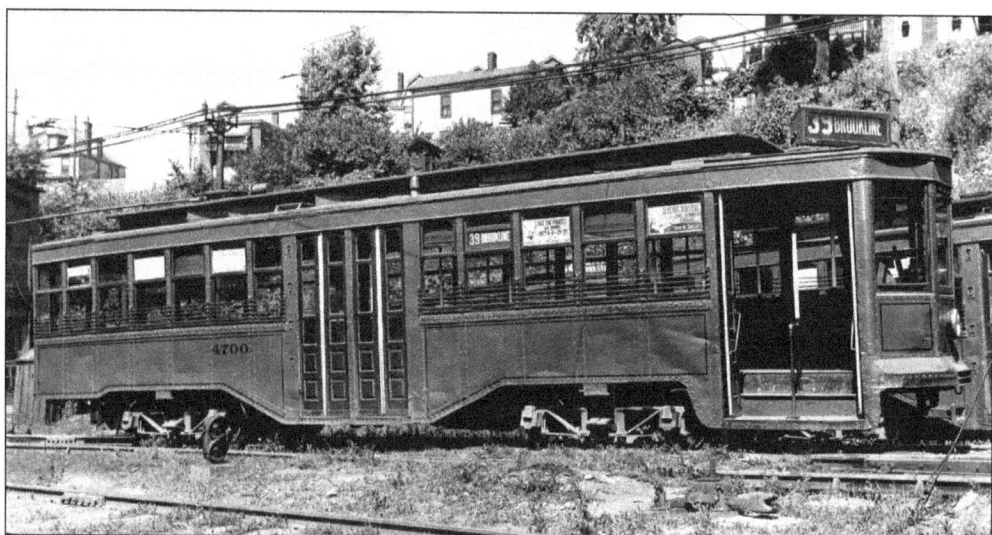

Seen at the South Hills Junction in 1948 is a Jones car, a 40-foot, double-ended, low-floor car of steel construction. Originally painted maroon with gold trim, the cars were painted "chrome orange" beginning in 1925. The company felt the new color would improve visibility of the cars in the increasing amount of motor vehicle traffic on Pittsburgh streets. The orange faded quickly in the Pittsburgh pollution to a yellowish color—hence the nickname "yellow cars." P. N. Jones, a Pittsburgh Railways superintendent from 1915 to 1927, is credited with their design. The cars were the mainstay of service in Brookline from 1915 until the President's Conference Committee (PCC) cars were introduced in 1940. They were phased out in 1954.

The Tintelnots pose with their automobile in front of their Norwich Avenue home in 1927. Short pants, or knickers, were standard clothing for boys until they were teenagers.

This pre-1936 view of Brookline Boulevard shows the trolley right-of-way that was placed in 1905. Pavement ran to Queensboro Avenue.

A new PCC car is shown driving inbound at Brookline and Kenilworth in 1940, soon after the introduction of streamliners on the line.

Pictured in the late 1950s is the intersection of Brookline Boulevard and Kenilworth Avenue. The entire hill was private track when the line was first built. The city shifted Brookline Boulevard and paved it in 1936.

The new West Liberty ramp, shown in 1940, took the streetcars away from the Liberty Tunnels, which are out of view just around the bend. Built as a trolley ramp in 1939, it was rebuilt by the Port Authority of Allegheny County and opened for bus traffic in 1977 as part of the South Busway project. Trolleys were replaced by buses of Route 41D in 1966.

Below Creedmore Avenue, tracks remained in the private right-of-way. All of Brookline Boulevard looked like this until 1936. No. 1697 inbound is shown here just past Whited Street.

A trolley travels up Brookline Boulevard toward Edgebrook Avenue from Whited Street. The trolley was chartered by Barry Goldwater supporters in preparation for his presidential bid in 1964. Streetcars were available for charter by private parties for tours and other functions, similar to limousine service today. This photograph was taken by John Bromley.

PCC car No. 1408 sits at the loop at Brookline Boulevard and Witt Street in the early 1960s. The operator is punching the headway recorder mounted on the pole. All operators punched in when they arrived and left the loop. The recorder was connected to the Pittsburgh Railways Company's main dispatcher, who could tell whether service was operating properly by the signals received.

A panoramic view of Brookline Boulevard at the top of Stebbins Avenue shows the inbound trolley and the automobiles of the day. The landscape itself has not changed much since this 1960s view.

Taken near Pioneer Avenue in 1965, this photograph shows a "Car Stop" sign attached to the electric wires that ran the trolleys.

Two trolleys pass on Brookline Boulevard as an automobile sneaks between the inbound trolley

and the parked cars near Stebbins Avenue in 1965.

This view is looking up the Boulevard from Queensboro Avenue in 1965. Triangle Park, housing the Brookline Monument (known as the Cannon), sits on the left. Gas prices were a little lower back then, as can be seen on the Mobil sign. A CoGo's convenience store now occupies that corner at Glenarm Avenue, and the gas pumps have been removed.

This is the Downtown Motors Pontiac dealership, on West Liberty Avenue. The Pontiac Company was created as a part of the G.M. Corporation in 1926. It became one of the leading brands of cars in total sales (second behind Chevrolet). The dealership was recently torn down to make way for the expansion of another dealership.

Four

BROOKLINE BOULEVARD

In the early 1900s, Brookline Boulevard took shape, starting at West Liberty Avenue and present-day Bodkin Street. The streetcars used the Pittsburgh Railways right-of-way exclusively. This traffic pattern changed in 1935, when the right-of-way was widened and paved for vehicles.

Brookline Boulevard became the centerpiece of the community, a commercial district full of shops catering to the needs of the neighborhood. In time, the roadway was paved completely from West Liberty through to Edgebrook Avenue, leaving the lower portion as a two-lane road separated by tracks. In 1966, streetcar service was discontinued, and the Boulevard was widened to four lanes all the way through to Breining Street.

Through the early 1970s, Brookline Boulevard maintained the same makeup with a variety of stores, including several hardware stores (Fred's, Nolan's, Bryant's, Jay's), the Town and Country women's store, the Boulevard Men's Shop, Tryson's Shoe Store, the Sound Shed, three pharmacies (Charleson's, Brookline Pharmacy, and Stebbrooks), several individual doctor's offices, and numerous other service-oriented establishments.

The mid-1970s recession, the rise of the suburban malls, and the "superstore" swamped the small business owner and caused quite a shift in consumer tastes. Many of the small community stores went out of business as the public flocked to the new and larger megastores and to the comfort of the modern shopping malls. There was a noticeable shift in the types of businesses located on the Boulevard. Empty storefronts were a problem that threatened to undermine the community. Through the efforts of many concerned citizens and community groups, Brookline Boulevard survived the hard times and is well on the road to recovery.

Today, Brookline Boulevard remains a vibrant commercial district, but the makeup of the stores has seen many changes. Rather than hardware stores, there are pizza shops. Instead of upscale clothing outlets, there are dollar stores. There are banks, barbershops, and beauty salons. However, the small community drugstore has been displaced by a large chain pharmacy, and in place of the local family doctor's office we see HMO family medical centers. Despite these changes, Brookline Boulevard is populated by businesses that offer a fine selection of goods and services, and it is possible to find great deals at many locations.

The Boulevard has always been and will continue to be the center of activity in the community, the hub around which Brookline will revolve into the 21st century.

The Brookline Firehouse was built in 1909 at the corner of Castlegate Avenue and Brookline Boulevard. Today, it is the oldest standing engine house in Pittsburgh. The original crew of city firefighters who manned the station used the lookout tower to spot fires and responded with a horse-drawn wagon with a steamer pump. Fire hoses were hung to dry from the crow's nest. The crow's nest lookout was replaced with mechanical call boxes located on street corners. These boxes remained in place until the 1980s, when they were replaced with 911 telephone service. Motorized transportation arrived in 1914, and since that time the community has witnessed a steady progression of new firefighters and new fire trucks. The engine house, however, has remained a constant, a silent guardian that roars to life whenever there is a threat of fire. It has seen some renovation over the years, but for the most part it is the same building that has served Brookline for nearly a century.

Pictured in 1936 are storefronts on the 500 block of Brookline Boulevard near Pioneer Avenue. These buildings were razed in 1999 for construction of the CVS Pharmacy.

This photograph was taken from the other end of Brookline Boulevard in 1936. It is a bustling view with autos, trolleys, and pedestrians.

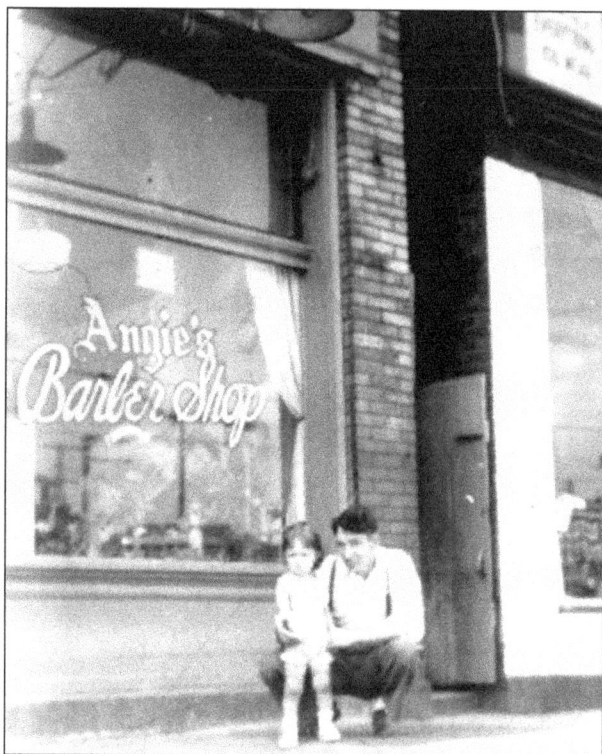

Angie Capuano poses with his oldest daughter, Mary Lee, in 1937. The construction of 956 Brookline Boulevard was completed in 1915. Angie and his family moved in when he was eight months old, and he lived there until a few months before his death in 1994. His parents, Vincent and Mary Capuano, built the building, which was one of the very first on Brookline Boulevard. There were five children—Lena, Joe, Angie, Franny, and Red. Vincent ran a shoe-repair shop on the first floor until his death in 1941. Red then took over the shoe-repair business until 1970. Five generations of Capuanos lived in the building, which was sold to the current owners in 1994.

The Cunocar was a traveling accounting and bookkeeping service run by Robert Rebel and Gerald Wickman, shown here in 1946 on Brookline Boulevard in front of St. Mark Church. Both started as tellers at Brookline Savings Bank before joining and starting this business. Their office was located at 908 Brookline Boulevard, above Boulevard News.

The Brookline Monument has been Brookline's most identifiable landmark for nearly 70 years. No one is sure exactly when the monument was dedicated in Triangle Park (at the corner of the Boulevard and Queensboro and Chelton Avenues), but everyone in this community knows the Cannon. The present monument is actually a replacement. The original World War I artillery piece was donated by the American Legion to the J&L Mill in Hazelwood to be melted down during a scrap-metal drive for World War II. It happened on October 13, 1942, when John Renner (a roller at the J&L 16-inch roller) and George Winslow (superintendent of the mill's Hazelwood polishing plant and senior vice commander of the Brookline Legion Post 540) held a small ceremony before the 4.7-inch cannon was again carted off to war, this time against the empire of Japan. The cannon was inscribed, "To Japan via U.S. armed forces."

Fred and Agnes Daley opened the Park Side Grill in 1948. Fred was an architect who designed the building and restaurant. Once located at 1017 Brookline Boulevard, it was the popular spot for young people to meet and have a bite to eat until 1965, when Agnes Daley retired from the restaurant business. Their son Bob now owns his own business at that location, South Hills Art Center. A number of Brookliners who grew up in the 1950s and 1960s still get together at South Park for an annual picnic to reminisce about those days and stay current with each other.

The Pittsburgh area's worst snowstorm began on November 25, 1950, dumping a record 30^1/$_2$ inches of snow in Brookline. Because of the large amount of snow and stranded vehicles, downtown Pittsburgh was not open to all traffic until December 1. This photograph shows 808 Brookline Boulevard when it was the Boulevard Gardens movie theater. Today, it is the Cedars of Lebanon meeting hall.

Brookline's new post office building, where it currently resides at 612 Brookline Boulevard, was dedicated on October 9, 1958. Prof. Joseph Moore (left) and Congressman James Fulton stand at the podium.

Charles Guest, superintendent of the Brookline Branch Post Office, cuts the ribbon at the dedication ceremony. Behind him are, from left to right, C. R. Mussetter, Thomas Gallagher, and Father Maynard.

Charles Guest and two postal employees pose for a photograph inside the post office.

Brookline's longtime local newspaper, the *Brookline Journal*, was published by Dale Noah for 49 years. It was a much anticipated weekly publication that covered a wide variety of events, stories, and issues relevant to Brookline. Noah, through his years of dedicated service to the community, endeared himself to the citizenry. There has not been a regular Brookline publication since the *Brookline Journal* ceased operation in 1982. It is interesting to note that some of the same issues in this 1964 sample remain of concern today.

Jacob and Dorothy Kribel started Kribel's Bakery on Troy Hill on Pittsburgh's North Side in 1933. They purchased the building at 546 Brookline Boulevard in 1946. An addition was built that tripled the size of the operation. Their four children purchased the business in 1974. Two of them and their families, Jacob and Lesley Kribel and Maxine (Kribel) and Richard Kaminski, still own the business today. This photograph of the facade was taken in 1967.

Brookline Boulevard has a long tradition of satisfying the sweet tooth of its residents via bakeries like Party Cake, Blue Bonnet, Kribel's, and Kuntz. Here patrons peruse the daily assortment of baked goods at Party Cake.

Leo Demma started working here at the age of 15. After his service to our country, he came back to Brookline and purchased the business, naming it Demma's Market, located at 934 Brookline Boulevard. He employed the previous owner for a time. Leo and his wife, Rose, are pictured inside the market below. Rose would help out on weekends and when employee vacancies needed to be filled. They sold the business in 1985.

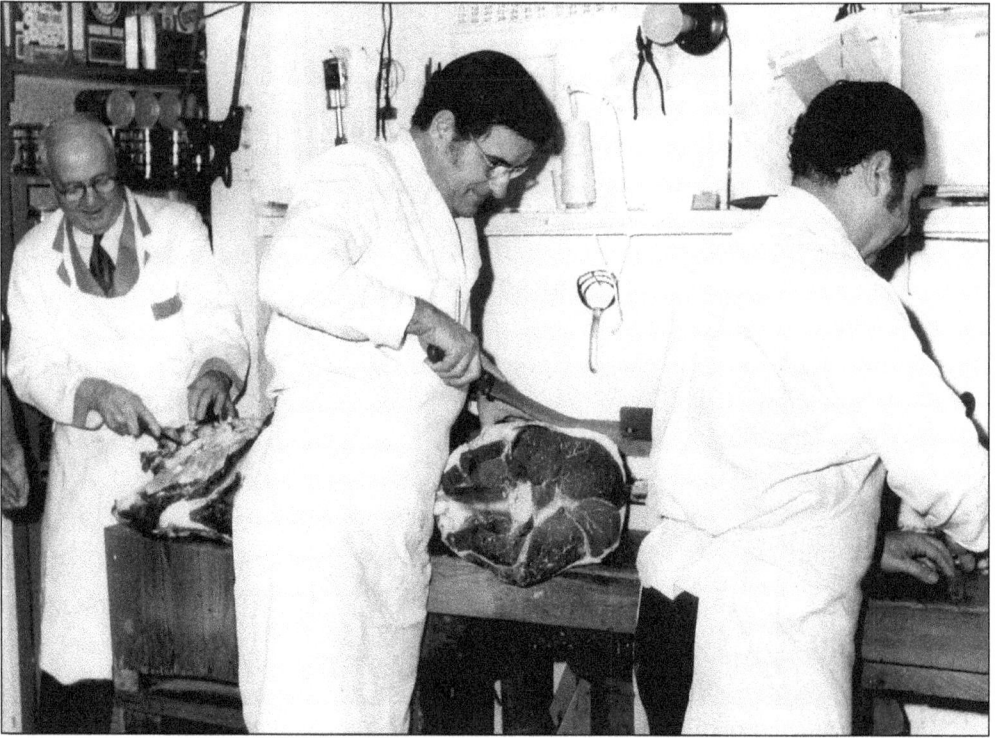

The butchers at Demma's Market in 1973 are John Seiler, Leo Demma, and Dom Coricelo.

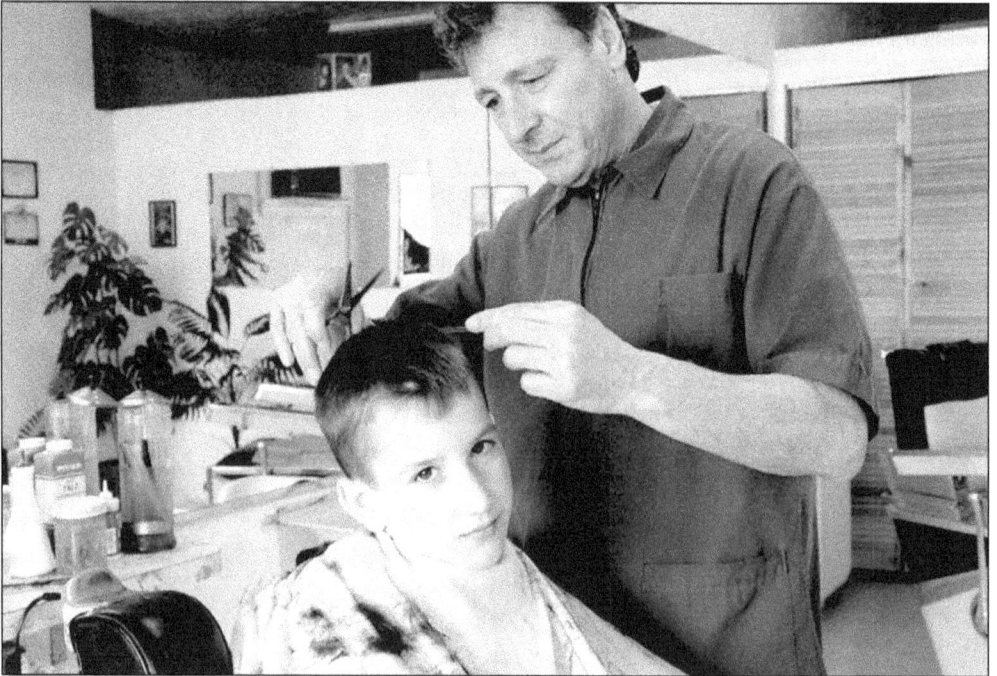

Here is just one example of the many barbershops and beauty salons that have always dotted Brookline Boulevard and continue to thrive today.

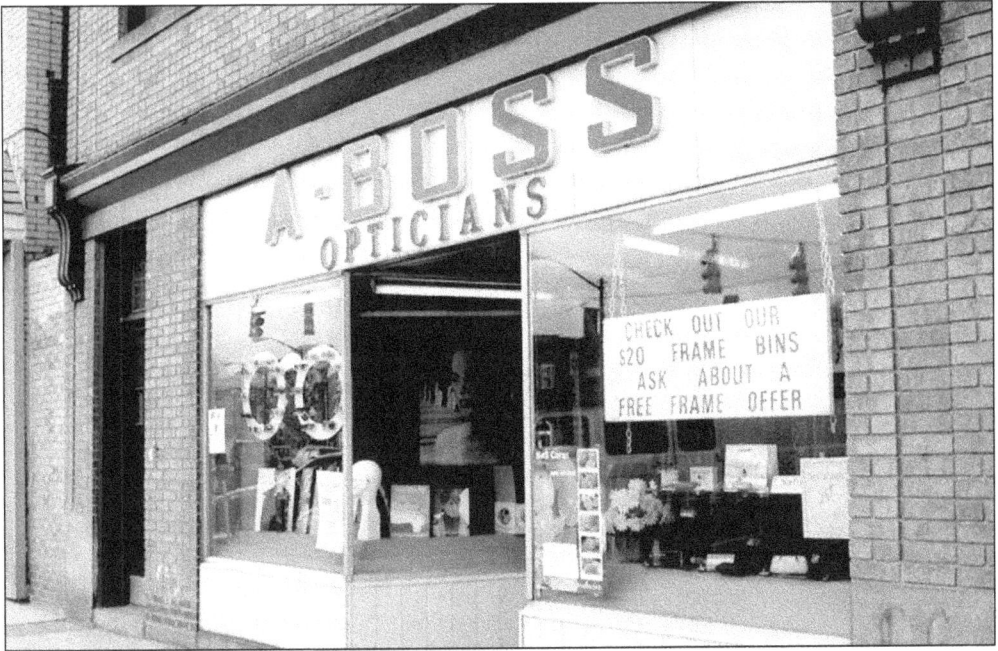

Albert Boss started A-Boss Opticians in 1971, replacing Dr. Myers's optometry business at 938 Brookline Boulevard. His original location was in Braddock, but they lived on Berkshire Avenue, and because people regularly came to them for glasses, Boss opened the Brookline location. His daughter Linda currently runs the shops.

This image offers a unique view of the Cannon aimed up Brookline Boulevard.

The American Legion building (far left) is the only one that remains out of this row. The entire corner Brookline Boulevard and Pioneer Avenue is now occupied by a CVS Pharmacy.

Isaly's—the Pittsburgh ice-cream icon and creator of the Klondike bar, the Skyscraper cone, and chip-chopped ham—was a popular Brookline business. Melman's Market was also well known to the community. These 1988 Michael Haritan images are from a 24-photograph panorama of the entire length of the business district. That seems recent, but already much has changed. Haritan believes you should document some semblance of the community in various stages for the purpose of future generations.

Brookline Boulevard bustles with activity on a busy afternoon.

This mural greets visitors on Brookline Boulevard near Pioneer Avenue. Community volunteers such as Ruth O'Hanlon, Elva McGibbeny, Alice Doran, and Marlene Curran led the Brookline Area Community Council to grand achievements in the 1960s. The council is a volunteer organization representing the community voice with elected officials and local agencies. This mural is one of its recent projects.

A trolley moves along Brookline Boulevard in 1966. The State Store is still in the same location (722 Brookline Boulevard), and the Premier Photo building is now the renovated Brookline Carnegie Library (708 Brookline Boulevard).

Five

EDUCATIONAL
INSTITUTIONS

The oldest school in the Brookline area was on Pioneer Avenue near Ray and Holbrook Avenues. Another school was located at the corner of Cape May and West Liberty. The East Side School, a frame building, stood on Edgebrook Avenue. There was also a private school at the south end of the present Liberty Tunnels.

In 1898, the West Liberty School was erected on Pioneer Avenue near the intersection with Capital Avenue. It was expanded in 1906. Overcrowding at the new school forced the school board to build Brookline Elementary School at Pioneer and Woodbourne Avenues. This modern four-room building was dedicated on July 4, 1909. Six rooms were added four years later, and six more were added in 1920. Another wing of nine rooms was built in 1929. In addition to the public schools, construction of Resurrection Parochial School began in 1909, and the first students attended in the fall of 1912.

Alice M. Carmalt Elementary was built in 1937 on Breining Street. St. Pius X Parochial School was erected in 1955 to ease overcrowding at Resurrection, and Our Lady of Loreto followed in 1961. Other educational institutions included DePaul Institute (built in 1910), a nationally renowned school for the hearing impaired, and Toner Institute, a military-type training academy for poor boys run by the Capuchin Fathers. Toner was chartered in 1941. Pioneer School was constructed as a special education facility.

The old West Liberty School was sold in 1938 to the Catholic Diocese of Pittsburgh for use as a girls high school called Elizabeth Seton. To replace West Liberty School, a modern school building was built at Crysler and LaMoine Streets, also named West Liberty School. The new school was expanded in 1959. West Liberty School was again closed in 1979, only to be reopened in 2000 after an additional new wing was constructed.

In 1996, in response to the financial difficulties of supporting three aging schools, the Catholic Diocese of Pittsburgh merged the three local parochial elementary schools—Resurrection, Pius, and Loreto—into one school named Brookline Regional Catholic, located in the old St. Pius School on Pioneer Avenue. The most recent addition to the Brookline school picture is South Brook Middle School, located in one wing of the Pioneer School.

Secondary public education for many years included but one choice, South Hills High School. The old school was closed in 1974 and replaced by the modern Brashear. For a parochial education, there was Elizabeth Seton (girls only) and South Hills Catholic (boys only), opened in 1960 and located off McNeilly Road. After the 1979 school year, the two Catholic institutions were merged to form Seton-LaSalle High School, located in the old South Hills Catholic building.

The eighth-grade class at Brookline School poses in 1913. James Addis is in front of the principal, to the right.

The sixth-grade class at Brookline School is shown in 1915.

The 1915 Brookline Elementary School varsity basketball team is pictured with the team pennant.

The Brookline School eighth-grade class poses in front of the school in 1917.

Children tend to the garden at Brookline School in the summer of 1916. School gardens were

used as a teaching tool and for sustenance, as the students' families benefited from the harvest.

Brookline School shown as it looked in 1928. The school, located at the corner of Woodbourne and Pioneer Avenues, was built in 1907. Work began on this school and one in the Beechview section of Pittsburgh at the same time. The two buildings were identical in design and size. Both were white-brick structures containing four rooms. Both schools were dedicated on the same day in June 1909. The first addition to Brookline School, designed by the architectural firm of Bartberger, Cooley and Bartberger, was erected in 1911. At the time this 1928 photograph was taken, a second addition, designed by E. M. Stotz, was completed.

The population explosion in Brookline caused Brookline Elementary School to become so overcrowded that classes were held part-time in 1928. The board of education made another addition to the Brookline building in 1929 at a cost of $106,000. At this time, the auditorium was rebuilt, and a kindergarten, two gymnasiums, and a cooking room were added. The photographs here show the construction of that new addition.

Alice M. Carmalt Elementary (shown here on July 28, 1937) was named in honor of the lifelong Mount Washington resident who served as a member of the original Pittsburgh Board of Education until her death. The school, designed by architect M. M. Steen and located at Breining and Georgette Streets, opened in June 1937. Originally an elementary school for kindergarten through fifth grade, it is now the Carmalt Academy of Science and Technology.

Elizabeth Seton High School on Pioneer Avenue, run by the Sisters of Charity, was formerly West Liberty Elementary School until the building was sold in 1938. It was dubbed "the Little Red School on Capital Hill" because it sits very close to Capital Avenue, a long and steep uphill climb from West Liberty Avenue.

West Liberty School, seen from Moore Park in the early 1940s, resembles a sentinel silently surveying the park's vast fields. Prof. Joseph Moore spent his life dealing with children, believing strongly the problem of juvenile delinquency could be best addressed by providing children with play areas. His efforts in this regard led to the construction of Moore Park in 1939.

A Brookline Elementary School music class is shown in this undated photograph. The school was used during the 1980s as a center for staff development and training for teachers who were temporarily transferred there for nine-week programs from all over Pittsburgh. The school also offered programs such as the SECTEM program (which focused on energy conservation) and was a Western Pennsylvania Conservancy Garden site.

Children at Brookline School observe the results of their Leaders in Defense stamp campaign in 1942. The Pittsburgh public school system was forced to adjust to national and international events during the 1940s. Following America's entry into World War II, Pittsburgh public schools began to offer civil-defense training to high school students. The schools also participated in the campaign to sell war savings stamps and bonds.

The Brookline School graduating class of 1944 poses for a photograph.

A student production at Brookline Elementary School depicts historical events during the mid-1940s.

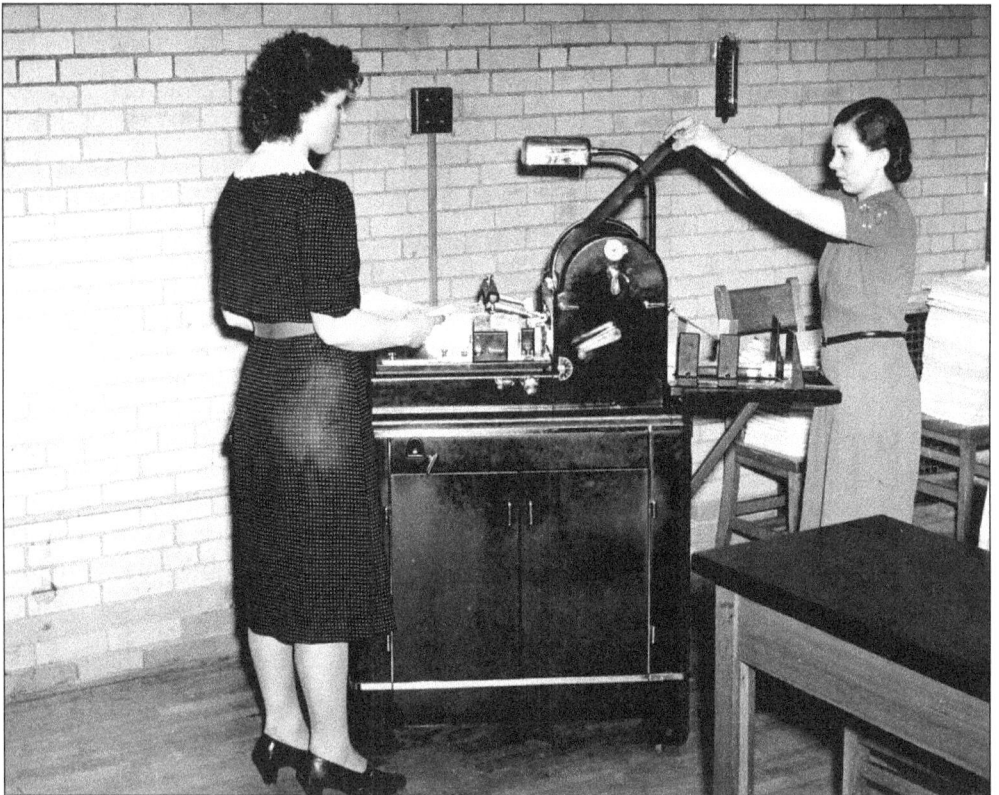

There were many learning opportunities available in Brookline schools. In this c. 1940s image, two ladies work a newspaper printing press for a school project at Brookline Elementary.

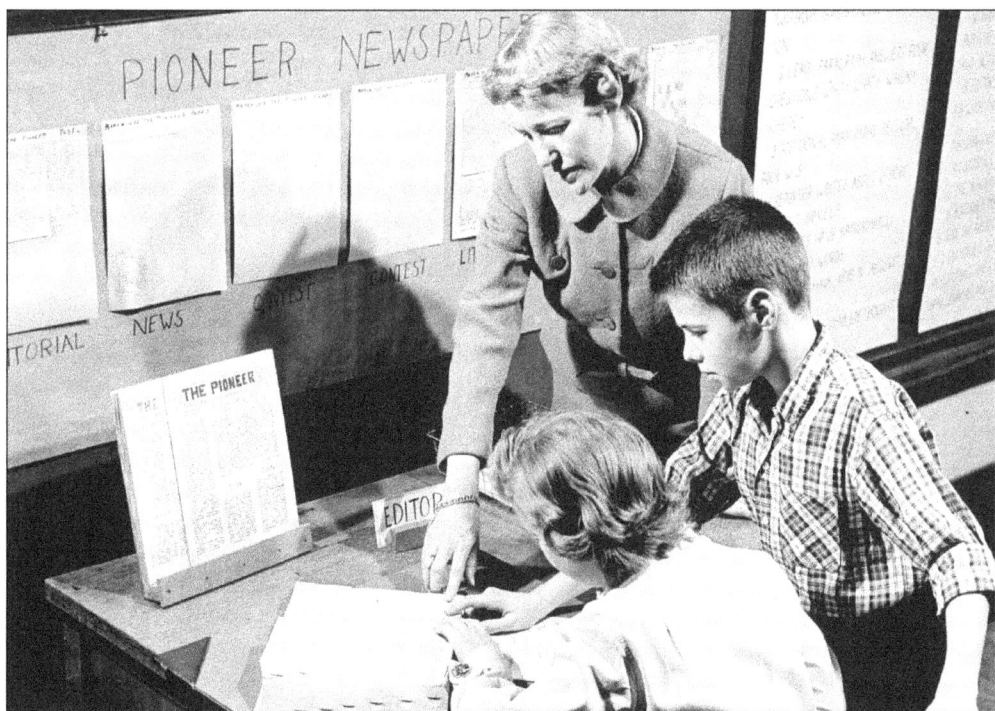

Brookline Elementary sixth-graders work on their newspaper, the *Pioneer*, in this 1958 photograph.

Sr. Mary Albans's 1959 eighth-grade class is shown at Resurrection Parochial School. Pictured are Dennis Flanigan, David Vietmeier, Wayne DeLuca, Joan Motznik, Ann Myers, Josephine Schuda, Noreene Genellie, Marilyn Lowe, Gerard Kilehm, James Nellis, Clyde Knorr, John Long, Timothy Boss, James Weber, Linda Gray, Carolyn Schultz, Janet Battle, and Harriett Nowakowski.

An aerial photographer took this picture of DePaul Institute *c.* 1960. It shows the density of Brookline to the left. The Catholic Diocese of Pittsburgh and the Sisters of Charity of Seton Hill founded DePaul in 1908. Originally known as the Pittsburgh School for the Deaf, it was located on Pittsburgh's North Side before it was moved to this building at the end of Castlegate Avenue in 1911. The school grew and prospered over the years. It served the needs of hearing- and speech-impaired students until 2003, when it moved to a larger location in Shadyside.

DePaul Institute is pictured here in an artist's rendering.

Michele Capuano (first row, second from left) is one of the second-graders shown in this 1954 photograph. She was one of 10 Capuanos who attended school at Resurrection. Baptisms, first communions, confirmations, marriages, and funerals were also conducted there. Many generations of Brookline families have a long history as part of the Church of the Resurrection.

Toner Institute
Home For Poor Boys

Chapel Of
Our Lady Of The Angels

Castlegate Avenue

South Hill Branch ♦ Pittsburgh, Pa.

Toner Institute, a school for poor boys, was run by the Capuchin Fathers. The school was chartered in 1941 and remained in operation until the mid-1960s. Located on the hill above Dorchester Avenue near DePaul Institute, Toner was a military-type academy, and the boys were taught the fundamentals of military drill and discipline while receiving a quality education. It was a common site at Brookline parades to see the finely dressed Toner cadets in formation in their West Point–style dress uniforms.

Six

CHURCHES

The first church in Brookline was at the end of Brookline Boulevard in an area where the people, sitting on stumps, would gather around the preacher to hear gospel stories. The Knowlson Methodist Church was erected in 1868 near the West Liberty Avenue and Brookline Boulevard junction on property bought from the late Richard Knowlson. In 1907, the church united with the Banksville Methodist Church. It was chartered in 1913, and a new church was constructed on Brookline Boulevard. The building is now home to the Brookline Assembly of God church.

A group of United Presbyterians had a small house of worship, erected in 1902, near the Bell House on West Liberty. In 1907, they moved to the West Liberty schoolhouse and then to the old Knowlson Church. They constructed their new church at Queensboro and Brookline Boulevard, dedicated on February 13, 1913, and enlarged it in 1953.

Resurrection Roman Catholic Church, known as "Ressi," was organized in 1900. Construction of a new school began in 1909, and the building was completed in 1912. From 1910 through 1939, mass was held in the basement of the school building until a separate church was built next-door on Creedmore Avenue. Over the years, the congregation at Resurrection grew to such proportions that a number of spin-off churches were formed, including St. Pius X (on Pioneer Avenue near McNeilly Road) and Our Lady of Loreto (on Crysler Street near Moore Park). Other spin-off congregations include St. Bernard's (in Mount Lebanon) and St. Norbert's (in Overbrook).

St. Mark Evangelical Lutheran Church was organized in 1906 as a mission in a small chapel on Bodkin Street (formerly Brookline Boulevard) with a membership of only 12 people. Its congregation flourished, and in 1928, a new church was constructed at the corner of Glenarm Avenue and Brookline Boulevard. The church was enlarged in the early 1960s and is the home of the Brookline Meals on Wheels program.

The Pittsburgh Baptist Church is located on Pioneer Avenue at the end of McNeilly Road. The congregation has been in existence since 1958 and has been holding services in the old Brookline church since April 1959. The church building, dating from the early 1900s, was originally the home of a Lutheran congregation, the Missouri Synods, and the sanctuary is steeped in Lutheran symbolism.

The Church of the Advent Episcopal was organized in 1904, and a small church was built on Pioneer Avenue near the intersection with Waddington Avenue. Additionally, there was the Paul Presbyterian Church, founded in 1923 at Dunster Street and Pioneer. The old church is now home to the Reformed Protestant Presbyterians. Our Lady of Victory Maronite Catholic Church was located on Dunster Street until 1997.

This is the Assembly of God church, on Brookline Boulevard. For many years, this was the home of the Brookline Methodist congregation. They were the first organized parish in the community.

The Flemings were early Brookline landowners with several acres of farmland along Pioneer Avenue. Elizabeth Fleming was an original member of the Church of the Advent Episcopal congregation who donated the land on which the church was built. Aidyl Avenue was named after her daughter Lydia, and the Port Authority of Allegheny County's Fleming stop bears the family name. St. Pius X is also constructed on lots purchased from the Fleming estate.

The Church of the Advent Episcopal began in the summer of 1904 in the home of Annie Johnston. A permanent church was erected in 1909 on Pioneer Avenue. Since that time, the congregation has grown and prospered. The church building was enlarged in stages over the years. In 2004, they celebrated their 100th anniversary. Below is a photograph of the sanctuary.

The Resurrection parish began construction of a new church and school building in 1909. The first floors of the building were completed by 1910. Services were held in the basement. The school was completed in time for the 1912 school year. The church floor was built of wood that buckled when it rained. Fr. Francis Quinn and church volunteers worked together to build a cement floor. The church remained on the lower floor of the school building until 1939, when the permanent church was built.

The Church of the Resurrection is a beautiful and highly ornate house of worship. Fr. Francis Quinn served here between 1909 and 1955.

Over the years, Resurrection has sponsored many groups and activities for the congregation. The children attended Sunday school and became members of the Boy and Girl Scouts. Many became altar boys or members of the choir. For adults, there were groups such as the Holy Name Society, pictured here on March 12, 1922.

The Pittsburgh Baptist Church sits on Pioneer Avenue at McNeilly Road. The building was originally built by a Lutheran congregation.

The United Presbyterian Church congregation acquired land in 1911 to construct a new place of worship. Purchased for $4,050, the existing structure, which is now considered the old chapel, was used for services while the main church was constructed. In May 1912, the congregation voted to change the name to the Brookline Boulevard United Presbyterian Church. The original cornerstone was laid on September 29, 1912, and the new building was dedicated on February 13, 1913. For the next 37 years, the church remained the same, with the old chapel and the new sanctuary.

The John Calvin Choir poses for a photograph at the United Presbyterian Church in 1960.

This is St. Mark Evangelical Lutheran Church c. 1960, before the construction of the addition that housed the community room and Sunday school. The home to the left of the church was the old parsonage and was used as such until a new home was constructed on Klein Place in 1958. Between then and the building of the addition, the home served as a Sunday school annex until it was torn down to make room for the new annex. The new structure was completed and dedicated in April 1964. Dr. Walter E. Miesel of St. Mark Church served from 1926 to 1953.

Marie Fisher Daugherty was the longtime organist at St. Mark Church. A master pianist, she also played for the Church of the Advent Episcopal, on Pioneer Avenue. The photograph is from the 1930s and shows the original organ at the new St. Mark Church, built in 1928. The beautiful organ was damaged and lost during a 1950s renovation.

St. Mark Church sponsors the "mini bus," a service for local senior citizens who need a ride from location to location. St. Mark is also home to the Meals on Wheels program, delivering hot meals to shut-ins.

This church dates from December 9, 1900. The first building used by the mission was located near the south entrance to the yet unheard-of Liberty Tunnels. A chapel was built in 1902 and was formally dedicated on June 11, 1903. Due to the growth of the area, the mission was relocated to West Liberty Public School in January 1907. A congregation was established a few weeks later, and services were held in the public school building until March 1908, when the "Knowlson M.C. Church" was purchased and renovated. At this time, the session was known as the West Liberty United Presbyterian Church.

Groundbreaking for Our Lady of Loreto Church and School took place on March 28, 1961. Clearing of the site began the following day. The site chosen was once a woodland area referred to as "Our Enchanted Forest." Seven acres were to be cleared for the new buildings. Four acres were to remain untouched, extending along the lower boundary of West Liberty School. On August 22, 1962 (the feast of the Immaculate Heart of Mary), dedication ceremonies were conducted by the Most Reverend John J. Wright. Attendance had to be restricted due to the limited facilities. The statue of Our Lady of Loreto, which had just arrived from Italy two hours before the ceremony, stood in the lobby and welcomed all. The entire cost of the new building was $541,650.

On May 25, 1984, a new hand-carved crucifix, pulpit, and altar, donated in memory of Msgr. James Shanahan, were installed in the sanctuary. On Sunday, May 27, on the 25th anniversary of the establishment of the parish, the altar (representing Christ with the family of Loreto) and the new lectern were dedicated by Father Chatt, dean of South Pittsburgh.

The cornerstone of the church and school was laid on August 21, 1955. On August 31, the new rectory was completed at 3059 Pioneer Avenue. On September 7, 1955, the school opened for the first time to the first through fourth-graders, and on December 3, Bishop Dearden dedicated the new church. The congregation included some 430 families. This photograph shows the church facade with the new relief of St. Pius X installed in 1988 and the bell tower.

Fr. Thomas M. Marpes was pastor for 34 years, from 1968 until his passing in 2002. The new activities building, Marpes Pavilion, bears his name.

Seven

LEISURE

Annually, the Brookline Board of Trade hosted a Fourth of July celebration featuring baseball games, races, a band concert, refreshments, and movies.

The first playgrounds in Brookline—at Gallion and Rossmore, Fordham and Norwich, and Aidyl and Pioneer—were privately owned lots. Residents were allowed to use them through the kindness of the owners. Additionally, a field between Whited Street and Milan Avenue was used as a recreation park, with a sandbox, swings, and slides and volleyball, monitored by teachers. Eventually these plots of land were sold, and the children were left without any space for playing.

Ground adjacent to Brookline School was to be used as a playground, but most of the property was used in the next school expansion. Prof. Joseph F. Moore, as chairman of the playground committee of the Brookline Board of Trade, became interested in acquiring and developing a plot along Pioneer Avenue as a playground site. This dream became a reality when the city council passed an ordinance that acquired and developed this land as a playground, now known as the Moore Recreation Center.

In the 1930s, Moore and the Joint Civic Committee also attracted the Carnegie Library to open a new branch on Brookline Boulevard. The first library was in the basement of the Brookline Methodist Church and, in the 1940s, was moved to a building at 730 Brookline Boulevard. In the 1980s, the library moved to 708 Brookline Boulevard, in the old Premier Photograph building. In 2003, the library underwent a total renovation, making it one of the Carnegie Library System's showcase community libraries.

As Brookline grew, the need for further recreational facilities arose. In 1945, the 20-acre Anderson Farm, in East Brookline, became available and was purchased by the Community Center Association in May 1947 for $19,000. Located between Breining Street and Brookline Boulevard, the newly acquired land was perfectly suited for a park.

The hilly terrain was excavated, and in 1952 the Brookline Little League began their inaugural season on the new baseball field. In 1966, the land was sold to the city for $1 with the promise that it would be developed into a city park. Forty years and several million dollars later, Brookline Memorial Park is one of the city's nicest community recreation parks. Moore Park also underwent some major renovations in the 1990s.

Finally, the Elizabeth Seton Center, on Pioneer Avenue, provides the community with recreation alternatives, including exercise facilities and daily lunches. Supported by the Sisters of Charity, the center offers child day care, adult day care, a full-service senior center, a music school, and a theater.

Prof. Joseph F. Moore (far left) and Will Saunders Jr. (second from right) march in Brookline's Fourth of July parade in 1929. Moore, the longtime principal at West Liberty, Brookline, and Carmalt schools, was a legendary figure in the community for over 60 years. He was a champion of free education, and his efforts led to the formation of the public school system.

Everyone loves a parade! Brookline has its share of festive occasions along the Boulevard. Fourth of July parades used to be held. Today, Brookline celebrates Memorial Day with a parade along the Boulevard and West Liberty Avenue.

Brookline's Girl Scout rifle troop participates in the Memorial Day parade in 1942.

This is another photograph of the 1942 Memorial Day parade. After the Civil War, Americans began to observe Decoration Day. It was a day to honor those armed services personnel who were killed during wartime. The holiday (now called Memorial Day) was named Decoration Day because the graves of the soldiers were often decorated with flags, flowers, and other memorial items.

The tradition of holding a Memorial Day parade dates from 1866. The town of Waterloo, New York, first organized a parade of veterans 100 years before Pres. Lyndon B. Johnson designated the town "the Birthplace of Memorial Day."

Around 1918, following World War I, Memorial Day became a day to honor all fallen American war soldiers from the American Revolution and beyond.

In 1971, Memorial Day began to be observed on the last Monday of May because of a 1968 federal law declaring it a national holiday and allowing employees a three-day weekend.

Memorial Day in Brookline always brings a great parade on Brookline Boulevard. Before the parade begins, a ceremony is held by the American Legion Post 540, at the Brookline Monument (known as the Cannon). The park is decorated with wreaths and flowers at the base of the American flag as a memorial to our fallen soldiers.

The Fourth of July parade assembles at the Cannon in 1961. Kids would join in the parade on bicycles decorated with bells and red-white-and-blue streamers on the handlebars. Red or blue playing cards placed in the wheel spokes would whistle as the kids rode along.

Moore Park's swimming pool in 1946 was the cool place to be on a hot summer's day. The Olympic-size pool featured a 16-foot-deep end with both high and low dive platforms, a concrete stand for viewing, and plenty of space for sunning and relaxing.

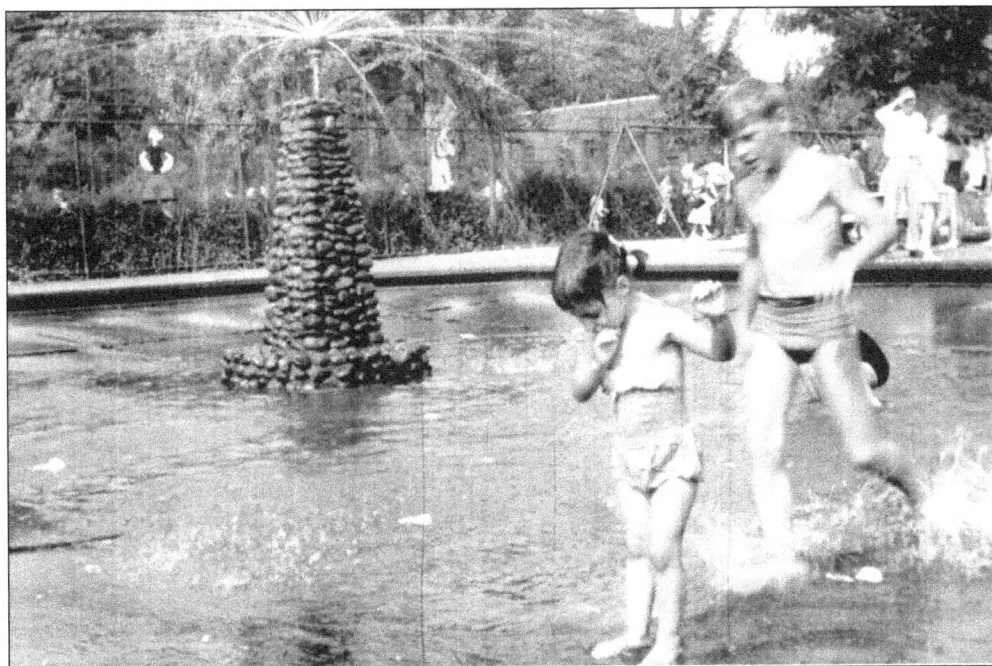

Sprinklers splash on a summer day at Moore Park's playground, where the reflecting pool preoccupies preschool-age Linda Dimitroff. Kids would cool off after a game of dodge ball or after playing on the swings, merry-go-round, and monkey bars. The sprinklers remain operational today.

Eleanor Esposito Dimitroff smiles for the camera in this 1960-era photograph, taken at Moore Park during the annual Fourth of July celebration, sponsored by the Brookline Chamber of Commerce. The hugely popular festivities kicked off with a parade down Brookline Boulevard and ended with fireworks at Moore Park. The daylong activities at Moore Park promoted family fun and included games, relay competitions, sack races, a water balloon toss, softball and baseball games, hot dogs, and ice-cream treats. At dusk, cartoon films and old-time movies were screened on sewn-together white sheets covering the infield fence along the lower ball field. The grand finale fireworks were set off from the woods on the downhill side of the ball field. The crowd sat on splintered, wooden-bench stands.

The Brookline Bowling League poses for a 1944 group photograph. Bowling was very popular at that time, and Brookline had two bowling alleys. One of them is still in existence under Cedars Hall, although it is no longer used. The other was under the current Banquets Unlimited building.

The Brookline Little League was chartered in 1952. The league consisted of four teams of 15 kids each, ages 9 through 12. Teams were sponsored by local organizations (the Brookline Memorial Community Center, the American Legion, the Kiwanis Club, and Ebenshire Village). There was also a traveling Pony League team, sponsored by Frank DeBor Funeral Home. The in-house season consisted of 18 games. The 1952 championship went to the Kiwanis team, led by Ray Auen Jr., Barton Christner, and Dennis Mangan, posting a 12-6 record. All-Star competition followed in the official Williamsport tournament. Shown here is a group photograph of the first bunch of Brookline Little Leaguers, managers, and coaches on the hillside at the new community center field.

The 1952 Brookline Little League All-Star team warms up at Moore Field for the game on July 4, 1952. They were victorious over Bethel Park 5-4. Brookline eventually lost to Brentwood in the district playoffs. The Brookline Little League Association was the dream of local merchants and baseball enthusiasts such as John Pascarosa, Morris Grummet, James McGaffin, and many others. These volunteers put Brookline baseball on the map and gave the local kids a place to play organized ball in a fun and competitive atmosphere. Men such as Sam Bryen, Angelo Masullo Sr., Ed Motznik, and Tony Colangelo continued the same work with the same dedication and leadership. It has been a rite of passage for over 50 years and one of the community's brightest assets. Brookline Boulevard's annual Little League parade is held each spring on opening day.

The Brookline Little League's traveling Pony team from 1955 posted a 28-0 record as undisputed champions of the South Hills. Manager Jim Klingensmith groomed the youngsters, resulting in a well-disciplined team. Their 28-game winning streak went unequaled in Brookline for 44 years, until the S. Poremski Plumbing Little League team of 1998–1999, coached by Tim Reitmeyer, went on a 31-game streak. Ironically, Tim's father, Harry, was a coach on this 1955 Pony team. Pictured, from left to right, are the following: (first row) Jim Nardo, Richard Mezyk, Bill Mulligan, Ronald Bua, George Cardone, and batboy Jackie Connors; (second row) coach Henry Hofbauer, Larry Valentine, Charley Watterson, Gerald Armento, Gary Wright, Bob Wertz, and coach Harry Conners; (third row) coach Harry Reitmeyer, Bud Auen Jr., Jimmy Klingensmith, Charles Mathias, Jimmy Lowen, Dennis Mangan, manager Jim Klingensmith, and team sponsor Frank DeBor.

The 1958 Little League All-Stars from Brookline won their first seven games en route to the District 4 city championship and then the Western Pennsylvania regional championship. Brookline was one game, one inning, and one run short of advancing to the official Little League World Series in Williamsport. This team finished second best in the state. From left to right are the following: (first row) Eddie Martin, Phil Dattisman, Denny Favero, Jimmy Savena, Greg Bailey, Jack Winters, and Jackie Flavin; (second row) Lou Blefere, Jack Wertz, Ronnie Bell, Dan Kail, Jack Emmerling, and Tom DeBasi; (third row) league president Sam Bryen, coach Herb Schiebel, Freddie Luvara, and manager Johnny Leaf.

Brookline players Jackie Flavin (left), Jack Wertz (center), and Fred Luvara are presented their District 4 city championship trophy by Pittsburgh mayor David L. Lawrence. The Brookline nine had just walloped the Perry Atoms 16-0 to claim the city title. Luvara was one of Brookline's top hitters, while Flavin and Wertz were the top hurlers. Wertz tossed a one-hitter against Perry in the District 4 title game and a no-hitter versus Hazelwood in the state semifinal to propel Brookline into the championship game.

The 12- and 13-year-olds of the 1978 Brookline Knights gather around coaches Rick Talerico (left), Bud Cambest (center), and John Boris to hoist their championship trophy. This was the first of many titles for the Knights football program, which began in 1974. The team was first organized by John Dowling and Jim Raimondi, and the winning tradition continues today under the leadership of 10-year president Joe Nicholas.

The Brookline Knights cheerleaders are shown in 1979, another winning season for the program. The 11-year-old Termite team went undefeated and captured their first championship. The girls cheered them on to victory in the final 20-10 win over Elizabeth-Forward. The cheerleaders include Nikki Marunich, Lisa Cambest, Colleen Hagen, Annie McDonough, Bobbilyn Mahoska, Debbie Pribik, Dawn Schilling, Lorrie Bova, Jennifer Dye, Judy Lutes, Mona Impell, Kelly Duggan, Chris Barth, Theresa Bruno, Tracy Murphy, Lorrie DiPippa, and Diane Stauffer. The girls were coached by Debbie Griffith, Patti Marunich, and Wanda Impell.

114

On July 1, 1961, members of the Kiwanis Club team from the Brookline Little League were treated to a special experience at Forbes Field. The defending world champion Pirates played Willie Mays and the San Francisco Giants. The boys met with Pirate manager Danny Murtaugh and several of the players, including Smokey Burgess, Don Hoak, and Roberto Clemente. In this photograph, left fielder Bob Skinner instructs, from left to right, Kiwanis teammates Pee Wee Esposito, Jackie Onodi, Danny McGibbeny, Kevin Jeswald, and Jackie Mitchell.

Maury Wills conducts a baseball camp with local kids at Moore Field. Wills was originally signed to play with the Brooklyn Dodgers as an amateur free agent in 1959. In 1962, while he was with the team, he was the National League most valuable player. He was traded by the Los Angeles Dodgers in 1966 to the Pittsburgh Pirates. He played with such Pirate greats as Roberto Clemente and Bill Mazeroski from 1966 to 1968. Baseball camp was a special day for the kids of the community, one that many still remember with fondness.

The 1968 pushball championship game was held at Moore Field.

Bob Dimitroff fields the ball at Brookline Memorial Park as a Little League player in 1970. Representing the city of Pittsburgh, Dimitroff competed and won the softball throw regional competition in the 1971 Jesse Owens Track and Field National Competition, held at the old Kezar Stadium in San Francisco. He ended up sixth nationally with a throw of 85 yards. He traveled to the competition with the other regional contestants, taking his first ever plane flight on this trip.

Danny McGibbeny succeeded in both professional sports and as a community champion. He worked in professional tennis management with the Pittsburgh Triangles of the World Team Tennis League. In three short years, he advanced to general manager and team coach, leading his tennis stars to the championship round in 1976. A year later, he died from cancer. Mayor Richard Caliguiri dedicated the newly built field to his memory in October 1977.

Danny McGibbeny grew up in Brookline and volunteered yearly as a coach with the Little League program. In February 1983, he was inducted into the Western Pennsylvania Sports Hall of Fame. In 1987, his father, Dan (a longtime Brookline resident and executive sports editor of the *Pittsburgh Post-Gazette*), was also inducted into the hall of fame. Together, the two Brookliners made up the only father-son duo at the time to gain entrance into the esteemed institution.

It is a fun day for the children of Brookline as the traveling merry-go-round visits at Chelton Avenue and Oakridge Street c. 1946.

In the 1960s, the Speicher family had an ice-skating rink, Brookline's first, on their property at 2324 Beaufort Avenue. Walt Speicher would block in the backyard when it was cold enough to create the rink. Later, they were caretakers for Brookline's second rink, created at Brookline Memorial Park.

Eight

PERSONALITIES
AND FAMILY ROOTS

Prof. Joseph F. Moore led the Joint Civic Committee in the 1930s in their efforts to modernize the Brookline area. The committee's achievements included the reengineering of Brookline Boulevard between Pioneer and West Liberty, the installation of street lighting, and the opening of the Brookline Branch of the Carnegie Library. In his later years, Moore became chairman of the Brookline Savings and Trust Company and was still active late into the 1960s. One of his final achievements was the construction of the new branch office of the U.S. Postal Service on Brookline Boulevard.

In 1951, John Pascarosa organized a group of Brookliners to form the Brookline Little League Association. From the meager beginnings of five teams fielding 80 players to today's multileague magnet that supports over 600 children, the Brookline Little League has been one of our community's brightest assets. Pascarosa was the first league president, but Sam Bryen became the "father of the Brookline Little League." Bryen's genuine love of children and his dedication endeared him to thousands of youngsters over his 25 years of service.

Two individuals have touched the lives of many Brookline children. Chuck Senft, who has served as recreation director at the Brookline Recreation Center since 1958. No man has worked harder to bring the kids of Brookline together and teach them the spirit of teamwork and dedication. Sue Moyer is remembered as the ageless school crossing guard at Creedmore Avenue and Brookline Boulevard. The image of her striding out into traffic, putting her hand in the air, and shouting, "Okay, honeys, let's go!" is etched in the hearts and minds of 50 years of Resurrection Parochial School kids.

Suzie McConnell is a basketball phenomenon whose achievements include state championships with Loreto and Seton-LaSalle, All-American status at Penn State, gold and bronze Olympic medals, selection as a WNBA All-Star, and a current position as head coach in the WNBA with the Minnesota Lynx. From 1991 to 2003, she served as coach at Oakland Catholic. Her teams posted a 321-86 record and three PIAA championships.

Brookline resident Craig "Porky" Chedwick, the self-proclaimed "Daddio of the Raddio" and "Platter-Pushin' Papa," became a radio legend in the 1940s and 1950s. The Boss Hoss still blows the dust off the oldies to this day, spreading the platters that matter over the airwaves for all of his loyal listeners. In 1998, Pork the Tork was inducted into the Rock and Roll Hall of Fame.

This chapter is a tribute to the famous and not-so-famous people who helped make Brookline the family neighborhood it is today.

The Kapsch family lived at 1114 Milan Avenue, where this photograph was taken in 1909. Pictured here are the first five children of Joseph and Amelia Kapsch: Amelia (Molly), Marie, John, Joe, and Josephine. Joseph came to the United States in 1902, and Amelia came in 1904 from Europe, settling in Brookline in 1906. Their other six children were Theodore, Leonard, Agnes (who married Fred Daley and later owned the Parkside Grill), Alfred, Lillian, and James. They farmed like so many people did in those days in what was at that time rural Pittsburgh. They had chickens and livestock and grew most of their own fruit and vegetables. When the Resurrection parish started in 1909, the Kapsch family was one of 12 families listed in its original membership rolls.

The Nagy family—Theresa, Ray, Steve Jr., Jim Nagy, and Steve Sr.—resided at 739 Dunster Street, as evidenced by this photograph taken in the 1940s.

Betty Meredith, LaVern Gerhmann, Betty Church, and Thelma Simpson pose in their Sunday best in the front yard of the Esposito's home during the mid-1940s. The Espositos migrated to their home on Plainview Avenue in Brookline from a crowded row home on the bluff near Mercy Hospital and Duquesne University in 1930. The girls were great friends since their first day of kindergarten in 1931 at the old West Liberty School. They retain and renew their friendship during their annual eighth-grade reunion held in Pittsburgh.

Elva Schragg poses for a photograph on Easter Sunday 1946. Her family lived on Plainview Avenue, the same street she lived on after marrying Pete Seaman. They had two daughters, Nancy and Barbara, who reside locally with their families. Elva was active at St. Mark Church, with Meals on Wheels, and with the Girl Scouts. She also raised ducks and dogs in her backyard. Elva was one of three passengers and the bus driver who were killed instantly in the horrific Brookline bus and trolley collision at the South Hills Junction on February 10, 1978.

Lawrence Voith Sr. holds his baby son, Ray, in their backyard at 1544 Berkshire Avenue. Lawrence worked as an accountant for the Jones & Laughlin Steel Company. He passed away in 1978. Ray's mother died in 1988. This is a typical view of the rear of a Brookline house and yard. Most homes were built along hillsides, with the home sitting above the hill or below it. The Voith family kept a lavish garden.

Two-year-old Ray Voith, his three-year-old brother Larry, and their best pal and next-door neighbor, three-year-old Hale Jenkins, sit on the porch step at the Voith home, at 936 Fordham Avenue. As they grew up and married, the Voith children moved into homes in the Brookline neighborhood, staying close to the original family homestead on Bellaire Avenue.

Ray Voith is shown with his grandmother on the day of his first communion.

Dorothy Voith poses on her bicycle for her father's camera.

Ray Voith washes his car outside 809 Bellaire Avenue.

Kathyrn Choby pulls Edward Choby Jr. on a sled near their 804 Bellaire Avenue family home. Sledding has always been a popular pastime for the children after a heavy snowfall. Several neighborhood streets were well known for their steep drops. Some of these were Bellaire, Flatbush, Stebbins, Castlegate, and Birchland.

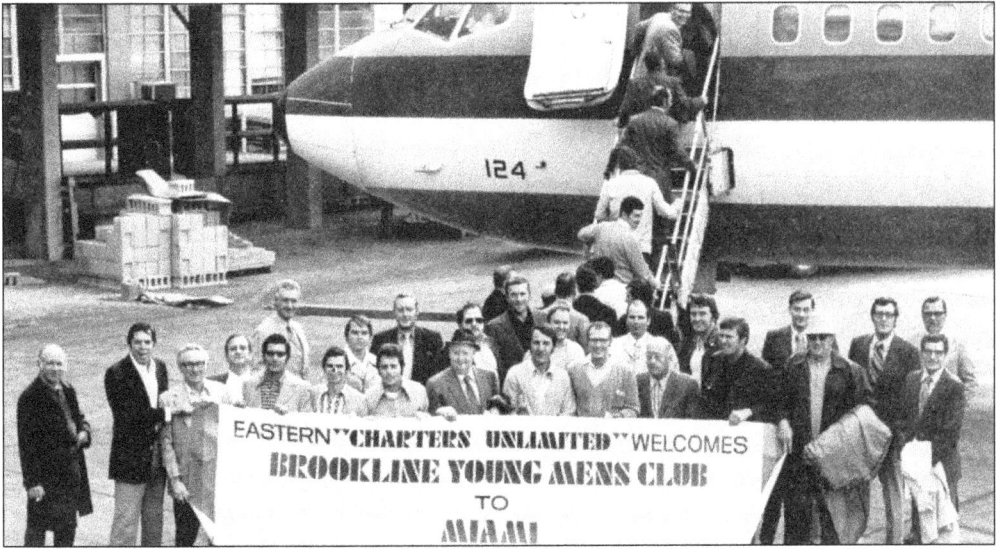

Angie Capuano opened his barbershop on Brookline Boulevard in 1936 and ran it until 1965, when he opened the Brookline Young Men's (BYM) Club. He sold the club in 1976. This picture shows the BYM Club during a trip to Miami, Florida.

Elva and Dan McGibbeny, longtime Brookline residents, are pictured on the night Dan was inducted into the Western Pennsylvania Sports Hall of Fame in 1987. A sportswriter for the *Pittsburgh Post-Gazette* and *Sun-Telegraph,* he joined his son Danny, who was inducted posthumously in 1983. Dan also covered Little League baseball under the name Mas Neyrb (Sam Bryen in reverse) in the *Brookline Journal,* publishing weekly write-ups on all the local games. Elva was also an active member of the community, holding the presidency at Brookline Area Community Council for many years.

The American flag flies proudly above the Brookline Firehouse as we look forward to a future as prosperous as our past.

www.ingramcontent.com/pod-product-compliance
Lightning Source LLC
Chambersburg PA
CBHW080603110426
42813CB00006B/1389